MW01131085

THE
DRAGON
OF BOEOTIA

MONSTERS OF MYTHOLOGY

25 VOLUMES

MONSTERS OF MYTHOLOGY

THE
DRAGON
OF BOEOTIA

Bernard Evslin

CHELSEA HOUSE PUBLISHERS

New York   New Haven   Philadelphia

1987

EDITOR
Jennifer Caldwell

ART DIRECTOR
Giannella Garrett

PICTURE RESEARCHER
Sarah Kirshner

DESIGNER
Victoria Tomaselli

CREATIVE DIRECTOR
Harold Steinberg

Library of Congress Cataloging-in-Publication Data

Evslin, Bernard.
The dragon of Boeotia.

(Monsters of mythology)
Summary: A fierce dragon plaguing region of
Greece comes into combat with the young
prince, Cadmus of Phoenicia.
1. Dragons—Juvenile literature. 2. Cadmus
(Greek mythology)—Juvenile literature. 3. Mythology,
Greek—Juvenile literature. [1. Dragons. 2. Cadmus
(Greek mythology) 3. Mythology, Greek] I. Title.
II. Series; Evslin, Bernard. Monsters of mythology.
BL795.D7E97   1987   398.2′454′0938   87-750

ISBN 1-55546-246-4

Printed in Singapore

For my grandson

LUKE BURBANK

whose eyes, fathom–blue, draw us deep.

Characters

Monster

The Dragon of Boeotia	A self-made monster; also known as Abas the Abominable

Gods

Zeus (ZOOS)	King of the Gods
Hermes (HUR meez)	Zeus's son; the Messenger God
Hades (HAY deez)	God of the Underworld
Poseidon (poh SY duhn)	God of the Sea
Demeter (DEM it tuhr)	Goddess of the Harvest

Hephaestus (hee FEHS tus)	The Smith God
Prometheus (proh MEE thee uhs)	The Titan; born of the gods; a friend of mankind
Atropos (AT roh pohs)	Eldest of the Fates; Lady of the Shears; she cuts the thread of life
Lachesis (LAK ee sihs)	The second Fate; she measures the thread of life
Clotho (KLOH thoh)	Youngest of the Fates; she spins the thread of life
Ikelos (IHK uh luhs)	Son of Hypnos, God of Sleep

Mortals

Celeus (SEL ee uhs)	King of Eleusis
Abas (AH buhs)	Celeus's eldest son; crown prince of Eleusis
Triptolemus (trihp TAHL uh muhs)	Abas's younger brother
Agenor (AG uh nor)	King of Phoenicia; father of Cyllix, Phoenix, Cadmus, and Europa
Cyllix (SY lihx)	Agenor's eldest son
Phoenix (FEE nihx)	Agenor's second son
Cadmus (KAD muhs)	Agenor's youngest son
Europa (yoo ROH puh)	Agenor's only daughter

Others

Arachne (uh RAK nee)	Formerly a maid of Lydia; then the first spider
Two vultures	Employed by Zeus to torture Prometheus
The black goat	Foster sister of Zeus; companion of Cadmus
A brown heifer	Also helpful to Cadmus
The dragon-men	Born from the dragon's buried teeth
Sileni (sy LAY nee)	Minor gods of wood and glade

Contents

1

The Curse

bas, crown prince of Eleusis, was a cold, sly youth who liked to hurt people but wasn't allowed to because his father, King Celeus, was a kindly man. "All that will change when I take the throne," said Abas to himself. "I mean to be feared, not loved. And I *will* be king one day, and do what I like to those I dislike. I can't wait."

But expectations, even princely ones, sometimes turn sour. And this eldest son never did become king.

One day, while riding through the fields, Abas saw a figure in the distance. He heard a voice calling, "Persephone! Persephone!" It was a woman's voice, but unusually loud. Then he saw a tall figure striding toward him. He looked up in amazement. Even on horseback he came only to her waist. "I seek my daughter, little man," she said. "Have you seen her?"

Abas did not relish being called "little man," but she was much too big to get angry at.

"I am Demeter," she said. "Barley-mother. Goddess of Growing Things. My daughter is Persephone. She was out with her paintbox to tint the flowers, as she does every spring. She's a rosebud herself, the little beauty, but she's gone . . . gone. Please, have you seen her?"

"I regret to say I have not," replied Abas. "Perhaps you should look in the meadow yonder, where wild flowers grow."

"Thank you," said Demeter, and went off with long strides, but so gracefully she seemed to float. Her voice came trailing back: "Persephone . . . Persephone."

But now that the goddess had left, Abas allowed his spite to boil over. "Persephone! Persephone!" he yelled jeeringly. "Come home; your mother wants you!"

Suddenly a huge screaming filled the meadow and glade— a savage gust of sound that made the horse buck and sent Abas flying off its back. He scrambled up and saw Demeter looming over him. Her hair was loose, her eyes blazing.

"Perhaps you should look in that meadow yonder, where wild flowers grow."

"Do you mock me?" she gasped. "Do you mock a mother in her grief? Do you jeer at me, Demeter, Mistress of Crops, who decrees famine or plenty, as I will? Do you dare?"

Her great hands gripped each other, and Abas shrank away, thinking she was about to pluck him off the ground and squeeze the life out of him. But she only pointed her hands at him, mumbling.

He felt her voice enter him. He felt his body tighten. It was a weird constriction, as if, indeed, a great pair of hands had seized him. But the goddess still had not touched him; she just pointed at him and mumbled. Abas felt himself dwindling. His chin hit something. It was his foot. A different kind—three-toed.

It had rained that morning, then cleared. Abas was beside a furrow that had caught some water, and he saw himself mirrored. He was tiny, green, jointed, polished—tapering to a whip of tail at one end and a head, very narrow, at the other. He stared at himself through popping eyes as his tongue flicked with marvelous speed. He watched that tongue wrap around a fly and draw it into his mouth. And he, who had always loathed the uncleanness of flies, felt himself devour one with gusto.

He looked up. Demeter was looking down at him. He was pressed against the earth by the wind of her voice.

> Lizard you are,
> lizard shall be
> Scuttle away,
> and remember me.

From that terrible day on, Abas lived as a tiny green reptile. This was particularly hateful to him, for while he had a lizard's body, he still had a human brain ticking inside his little leathery skull, and all his memories were intact. This is exactly what Demeter had intended, for it made his punishment infinitely more painful.

. . . tapering to a whip of tail at one end and
a head, very narrow, at the other. . . . From that
terrible day on, Abas lived as a tiny green reptile.

The lizard who had been a prince didn't know what to do. He thought of trying to find Demeter, to plead for her forgiveness. But, remembering her grief and rage, he knew that the goddess would never forgive him, that he was locked in his horrid little reptile form forever.

"No," he thought, "I don't want to live this way. I'll starve myself to death; I'll catch no more flies."

Nevertheless, as soon as he got hungry, Abas found himself waiting in the dappled shade where he was hard to see, his tongue flicking, catching insects and eating them until he was hungry no longer. He couldn't help it; hunger made him forget everything except getting something to eat. But as soon as his belly was full, life became intolerable again.

"I don't seem to be able to starve myself," he thought. "So I'll try another way. I'll let one of the things that hunt me eat its fill too. I won't scuttle away. I won't climb a tree or dive down a hole. I'll just stay where I am and be eaten. One moment of dreadful pain and I'll be gone, saving myself years of suffering."

So the next time the shadow of wings fell upon him he held his ground and let the hedge-hawk stoop. But just before the great claws struck, his animal nature took over. Flight possessed him. And he was gone, gone in a flash, whipping away from the hawk's claws, and disappearing into the long grass.

All this time, without being aware of it, Abas had been making his way back toward the palace grounds. Finally, he found himself in the royal garden. It was pleasant among the roses and there were beetles and bees to eat. On the third day of his stay, he overheard a conversation between two gardeners that sent him into a frothing green fit. His father, he learned, had been badly wounded in battle and was now lying in the palace on the verge of death.

"Just exactly what I've been waiting for all this time," Abas moaned to himself. "Why couldn't the old fool have gotten himself knocked on the head a little sooner? Then I'd have been hanging over his bed, pretending grief, instead of riding out in the damned fields, meeting that accursed goddess, and being changed into this loathsome thing that I am. But no . . . father had to wait until I was a lizard, and then get his stupid head beaten in. Now that brother of mine will inherit the throne. That simpering, goody-goody Triptolemus will be king!"

Raging to himself, he slipped into the castle, slithered up the wall, and crawled out among the rafters. He crouched on a beam above the royal bedstead and watched his father dying. His brother was beside the king, weeping.

"Look at him, squeezing out those tears," muttered the lizard to himself. "What a hypocrite! As if he could be anything but ecstatic at the idea of being king in a few days. I hate him."

But as this third son sat in the garden
planning his tame future, he had no way of
knowing that matters were being decided in high places.

Hunting was good among the beams of the old palace. Spiders had been busy there, and the lizard robbed their webs and ate their flies; any spider who came to object was also eaten.

And he who had waited so impatiently for his father to die

now wanted him to linger on because he could not bear the thought of his younger brother becoming king.

Our story now crosses the Middle Sea to its eastern rim, where flourished the rich and powerful kingdom of Phoenicia. Agenor, its king, had three sons: two of them were splendid young warriors, royally lethal. The eldest prince captained the war fleet; the second one commanded the army. But the third son, Cadmus, seemed unfit for war or peace. Runty, clownish, of barbed speech and odd tastes, he was a grief to his mother, a political liability to his father, and a source of rage to his brothers. Only his younger sister, Europa, cared for him, and she was the only one he had ever loved.

Cadmus knew that he would lose her soon. For princesses were married off early in those days, and since her father was very rich and she was very beautiful, the suitors had already begun to swarm about the royal palace.

"No, I shall not lose her!" Cadmus vowed to himself. "Her husband is bound to be a warrior, always out conquering someone. I'll keep her company when he goes off—gossip with her and tell her stories. And make myself useful to him, perhaps, by doing some of the clerkly things that kings hate to be bothered with."

But as this third son of the Phoenician king sat in the garden planning his tame future, he had no way of knowing that matters were being decided in high places that would plunge him into wild adventure, subject him to dreadful ordeal, and win him a place in legend forever.

1514

das ist albrecht dürer
muter dy was
alt 63 Jor

und ist verstorben
Im 1514 Jor
am erchtag vor
der crewczwochn
vij stvnd

2

The High Council

Zeus met with the high council in his throne room on Mt. Olympus. This council was composed of the three most powerful gods—Zeus himself, Poseidon, and Hades. There was a fourth member, Atropos, the eldest Fate. The withered little Scissors Hag sat wrapped in her fur cloak, for she was chilly even on the hottest days. She listened silently, never speaking unless spoken to. And she was never spoken to except in the form of a question, such questions being always about some twist of destiny, which the Fates alone understood. Her answers were always short, sharp, and precise. Everyone hated the Hag, but no one dared to cross her.

There was mighty business before the council this day, nothing less than the future of mankind. The gods had grown weary of the human race and wished to visit the earth with catastrophe—quake or flood or fire storm—to cleanse it of all life. Then, in time to come, they would permit the primal energies to express themselves anew in unobnoxious forms—as grass and trees, birds and beasts.

"We are beginning to repeat ourselves," said Poseidon. "We have punished humankind before, wiping them out even to the last verminous specimen, only to find them returning, crawling back into the life chain, disguised as fish, birds, monkeys, or whatever, then casting off fur and feathers to stride forth in all their pestiferous presumption."

"It is true," said Hades. "This has happened on two separate occasions. But I, for one, do not find such annihilation useless. My own kingdom has been considerably enlarged by these episodes."

"It's fine for you, brother," said Poseidon. "You simply sat there on your ebony throne waiting for them to join your realm, but I went to a great deal of trouble tearing the seas from their beds and hurling them upon earth. Now, only a few eons later, we're again having the same old discussion."

"On those other occasions," said Zeus mildly, "we acted without consulting our venerable cousin, and may unwittingly have run counter to the Master Design. She is with us today, however. Speak, Atropos. What do you say about our intention to exterminate the race of man utterly and for all time?"

"It is not written," said Atropos.

"Indeed?" growled Zeus, brows knotting.

The others watched uneasily as his huge hands fiddled with the lightning shaft that was his scepter. For they all knew that while Zeus spoke diplomatically about Destiny and Providence, which even the gods had to obey, he did not really recognize anything that did not serve his own intention.

"I pray you," he said, "clarify your objection, good Atropos."

"It is clearly stated in our Great Scroll that humankind enjoys a choice," she replied. "Man is to be destroyed only if he destroys himself. It is further written that such impulse for destruction shall arise from a humanoid race spawned by a dragon-to-be on a certain riverbank in Boeotia."

"Are you telling me that such dragon spawn will be more mischievous, more warlike than the present breeds of man? I find that difficult to believe."

"The mandates I serve, great Zeus, do not require your belief, only our performance. Know this, cousin. Man is warlike today in an innocent bestial way. He fights as lions do, or wolves, or stags in spring—for a piece of territory, a haunch of meat, first choice of mate. And when the purpose has been accomplished, the hunger fed, then the fighting ceases. But the future breed of man, the sons of the dragon, shall depart from such innocent animal ways and attach their killing instincts to ideas of virtue. A simple but profound change will occur in the way people think; by a lethal twist, murder will be viewed as a solution for all problems—and quite legal, if done properly."

"Imitating us again," muttered Poseidon. "And in our most godlike activity. Intolerable."

"May I continue?" asked Atropos. "Or ought I yield the floor to your moist majesty?"

"Your pardon, cousin. Pray continue."

"Thus, impelled by such ideas," said Atropos, "and having armed themselves with the primal fire, the nations of man will

"And having armed themselves with the primal fire, the nations of man will proceed to incinerate their enemies."

proceed to incinerate their enemies, that is, everyone else. But despite all their knowledge, they will not have learned the simplest lesson of fire—that it spreads—and so it will consume them as well."

"Most encouraging," said Zeus. "And all stemming from some future dragon, who will be a remarkable specimen, I presume?"

"Yes, indeed," said the Hag, "to be called Abas the Abominable."

"Aren't all dragons abominable?" asked Hades.

"This one more so," said Atropos. "But hearken, Zeus. There is something you must do before the dragon can play its role."

"Only you, dear cousin, may say 'must' to me," said Zeus.

"Be not wroth, my lord," murmured Atropos. "All important events must bear your royal imprimature; how else could they become important? And in the intricate designs of Destiny one event is linked to another."

"What must I do, my lady?"

"Something you will very much want to do—abduct the princess of Phoenicia, named Europa."

"And all this dragonish activity, the spawning of an even more warlike breed of man, and the destruction of humanity shall be the result of my coupling with this Europa—is that what you're telling me, oh Sister of the Shears?"

"Yes, your majesty."

"Is she beautiful?"

"Even the Fates, my lord, do not dare present you with an unattractive partner."

This was closer to levity than Destiny's crone had ever come, and Zeus knew that mighty changes must indeed be afoot. He adjourned the council and sent for Hermes.

When the messenger god reported to his father, they discussed plans for abducting Europa without arousing the suspicions of Hera, who was Zeus's wife, and savagely jealous.

"In these matters," said Zeus, "I have most successfully avoided detection through simple impersonations—as an eagle, a swan, a shower of gold, and so on . . . "

"What do you fancy this time?" asked Hermes.

"Well, according to Atropos, this will be a fateful abduction, heavy with consequence, so it would seem to call for something imposing."

"Imposing? Well, how about a bull, a huge white one with golden horns and hooves, and eyes like pools of molten gold?"

"Sounds good," said Zeus.

3

The Abduction of Europa

Prince Cadmus had wandered out of the royal garden and was walking along the edge of an orchard. He sat on a tree stump and let himself sink into the rustling silence. A bird called. He whistled. The bird replied. He saw something moving and chirped. A field mouse popped out of the grass near his feet, peering at him with bright beady eyes. Cadmus made a chittering sound; the mouse chittered back, and vanished.

"They whistle, they chirp," he thought. "Bark, roar, growl, howl, hiss, and sing. It's all speech of a sort, and can be learned."

A wind struck, rattling the leaves. It tore a piece of bark off a tree and sailed it toward Cadmus. It landed at his feet, and he picked it up. It was hard and wrinkled on one side, smooth on the other. He took a pointed twig and tried to draw on the smooth side of the bark. The marks were too faint to see. He drew his dagger and carefully pricked the ball of his thumb. It bled slightly. Dipping the point of the twig into the blood he started to make marks on the bark.

He drew an oval with two prongs coming out of it. "An ox," he said to himself. The word for "ox" in early Phoenician was *aleph*. "Aaaahh-lef," he muttered to himself. "The sign of the ox shall be the sound *ahhhh*, which should flash into memory every time this sign is seen. But there are so many sounds. Will I have to find a sign for each? Can I think of so many? And who will remember them if I do? Oh well."

Cadmus then drew a box standing on its end, with a figure inside. "That's a house, *Bet*. By the sign of the house, one shall hear *b-b-b-b*. So I have two—Aleph, Bet . . . not much, but it's a start."

Cadmus rose from the stump and wandered back through the royal gardens to the palace. The courtyard was in great tumult. But his mind was such a whirl of signs and sounds that he ignored the excitement and was passing through the crowd. His father's bellow shattered the air. "Ah, there he is, the little nitwit!" roared Agenor. "Dreaming his life away as the enemy comes ashore and steals his sister!"

"What, father? Who stole whom?" asked Cadmus.

The old man grew so red in the face that Cadmus thought he must burst like overripe fruit. The king clutched at his tunic and pulled it away from his neck so he could breathe. Cadmus had often enraged his father, but never like this. His brothers rushed to Agenor.

"Take him away!" gasped Agenor. "Take him off somewhere before I kill him. 'Who stole whom?' . . . Aggh!"

"Someone please tell me what happened," said Cadmus.

"Everybody knows but you," replied Cyllix, the eldest brother. "While Europa and her maidens were playing on the beach, someone or something came out of the sea and carried her off."

"What do you mean, 'someone or something'?" cried Cadmus. "I don't understand."

"Nobody does," said Phoenix, the second brother. "Those silly girls tell a confused story. They speak of a bull coming out of the sea, a big white bull. They say that Europa jumped on its back. That it rushed into the sea and swam away."

Cadmus had often enraged
his father, but never like this.

"Obviously, no bull," said Cyllix. "It must have been one of those northern pirates who wear horns on their helmets. One of them must have slipped ashore and carried her off. And the girls were too frightened to tell the difference."

"Very strange," said Cadmus. "Shall I go question the girls? Perhaps you frightened them."

*"While Europa and her maidens were
playing on the beach, someone or something
came out of the sea and carried her off."*

"Yes, let him question the girls," said his father. "What else is he good for? You two, gather your men and go search for your sister. Cyllix, sail westward with the fleet. Phoenix, take the army and march east. The abductors may have circled the headland and struck inland. And let this nincompoop stay here and question the girls and whistle at birds and chirp at field mice and chase his crazy dream of capturing speech in a tangle of magic marks—like a forester snaring birds with a net. Go, my brave sons, go. Pursue the abductor; save your sister."

"Father," said Cadmus.

"Get out of my sight!" muttered Agenor. "Oh, why couldn't someone have stolen you instead?"

4

The Lizard's Ambition

he king of Eleusis finally died, as the lizard who had been his son watched from the rafters. Then Abas decided to leave the palace.

"I'm *not* going to crouch under a rose bush in the royal garden and watch my brother accept the crown that should have been mine," he declared to himself. "I'll go out into the fields again and try to work up courage enough to let a hawk eat me, or go swimming and be caught by a carp."

Abas left the palace grounds and made his way to a nearby wood. It was a hot, brilliant day. A lion was feeding upon a fallen deer, growling over the raw bones. Abas balanced himself on a twig of an olive tree and watched.

"It's not that I mind being unhuman," he thought. "There's much about animals that's appealing. It's being a *lizard* that I loathe. I'd gladly put in time as a lion, for example—all blood and gold, roaring and springing, crunching bones, terrifying man and beast. Not a bad life at all."

Something blotted the sun. Abas looked up. His senses spun like a top. He thought he must be asleep, dreaming. Hovering above, shadowing the entire glade, was *himself*, but magnified, exalted—a giant lizard, armored in leather, with a ridged back,

A lion was feeding upon a fallen deer.

spiked tail, enormous jaws, and—to make it totally fearsome—
a pair of huge, ribbed, leathery wings.

It swooped low, the leaves flattened. Abas was almost
blown off his twig by the down draft. The monster opened its
jaws, spitting flame, striking the ground near the lion, who sprang
thirty feet in one leap and cowered at the other end of the glade.
The giant lizard swept up the carcass of the deer, then flew up
above the treeline, devouring the carcass in midair. It was gone

in three swallows. The monster hovered, blood dripping from its jaws.

The lion trotted back into the middle of the glade and stared up at the beast who had dared steal his meal. He roared. To Abas, watching, it seemed that the huge flying lizard responded as swiftly as a hawk spotting a field mouse. Its great body tilted toward earth and lanced down. It fell like a lightning bolt. The great hooks that were its claws struck the lion, grappling him tight. The leather wings beat the air, and the monster soared away, bearing the lion into the sky, like a hawk seizing a field mouse, or an eagle stealing a lamb.

He was remembering . . . seeing his father
ride into the courtyard in full battle gear.

Abas gazed after it into the blinding blue sky, not believing what he had seen. The glade was empty. But where the deer had been was a circle of scorched grass, so Abas knew that what he had seen was real.

He was in a swoon of adoration and wild hope. He felt almost as if he were human again, but a boy. Then he realized that he was remembering, and that the memory was of himself at the age of five, seeing his father riding into the courtyard in full battle gear. A big man, standing upright in a gilded bronze chariot, clad in gleaming bronze—breastplate, greaves, and eagle-plumed helmet, a sword at his side, a spear in his hand. The child watching him had thrilled in every fiber, promising himself that he would grow up to be a glittering bronze warrior king just like his father.

And now the little lizard was swept by the same feeling, but with greater fury. The magnificent creature that had snatched up the lion as if it were a mouse was a lizard also—shaped just like himself. Then, from the depth of his debased transformation, he would find a way to rise to the same splendor. Magnifying himself, growing wings, letting the flame in his heart kindle his breath. And so enlarged, so armed, he would avenge himself on the world that had humiliated him.

"That was a dragon," Abas said to himself. "Then there are such things; they're not just nursery tales. Very well, then, I aspire to be a dragon. Perhaps I'm a young one now, who can tell? After all, a butterfly begins as a caterpillar and grows

"Maybe a dragon starts small too."

wings later. Maybe a dragon starts small too. By the goddess who punished me, I welcome this transformation, and I shall not rest until I achieve dragonhood. Then, world, beware!"

Aflame with his vision, drunk with the power that was not yet his, the little lizard decided to go back to the palace and kill the newly crowned young king who was his brother. "I'll find a way," he thought. "Small as I am I'll finish him off, the lout, and show whoever needs showing that I'm dragon material."

5

The Titan

ow, there were two among the Immortals who loved mankind: an elder Titan named Prometheus and the young god Hermes. Hermes, however, was unable to help the human race; he was the messenger god, the favorite son of Zeus, and he had always obeyed his father in all things. While he was shocked and grieved when the High Council decided on the eventual destruction of the human race, he felt unable to do anything about it.

But Prometheus owed no obedience to Zeus. He had rebelled against one of the great god's edicts once, by giving man the gift of fire, and he was being terribly punished for it. Zeus had ordered him chained to a mountain crag and had sent two vultures to hover about him perpetually, driving their beaks into his belly and pulling out his great guts. Being of divine stock, Prometheus could not die, but he could suffer—and his suffering was meant to be eternal.

Despite his torment, however, he kept his courage high, and his intellect remained unclouded. He kept his love for mankind and his loathing for those who entertained themselves with the spectacle of human misery.

*When visiting Prometheus he became a giant
bat so that he could chase the vultures away.*

Such was the power of the Promethean personality that, condemned and helpless as he was, there were still those who venerated him and sought to serve him, despite terrible risk to themselves. Particularly attracted to Prometheus were some of the lesser gods, who were more intimate with human beings and didn't want to see them destroyed. One of the most fervent of these was Ikelos, a son of Hypnos, God of Sleep. He would change himself into a different animal every night. The most restless of Sleep's brood, he became a furry dream, the kind that prowls the margins of sleep. When visiting Prometheus he became a giant bat so that he could chase the vultures away for a while. But the big, bald birds would simply hover, wait until the godling was gone, then swoop down again, and tear at the entrails of the chained Prometheus.

This time, when Ikelos came, the Titan beckoned him closer so that he might speak to him. "I have an errand for you, Ikelos."

"Anything you wish, my lord, I shall seek to perform."

"Go to Phoenicia," said Prometheus. "Visit the sleep of Cadmus, third son to the king. Ask him to come to me."

"Yes, my lord."

"He won't know where to find me," said Prometheus. "Instruct him through vision, then lead him here."

"I shall go to Phoenicia this very night," said Ikelos.

6

On the Peak

Cadmus, asleep in the palace, saw a white bull swimming in a dark blue sea. Europa rode the bull, her hair swinging. Her face was hidden; he couldn't tell if she were happy or frightened. Now he was swimming after them. But this bull swam faster and became a tiny speck on the horizon.

Now Cadmus was swimming up a hill of water, not a wave or a swell, for it did not move, but a great cliff of water. Up, up, he swam; he was following a white fox; it was scampering up the hill before him. The wall of water became a dry hill, earth and rock; the foam on top became snow. Two ugly birds hung above, huge and foul. And when had it stopped being a dream?

The fox's tail was a plume of white fire; the animal turned and looked back at him. Its eyes were blue as the core of flame. Then it vanished, darting suddenly off the path among a welter of rocks, where Cadmus could not follow. He kept to the path, kept climbing. Far above a voice was thundering: "Cadmus . . . Cadmus . . ."

When he reached the top of the hill, he couldn't believe what he saw. A naked giant was slung between crags, chained to the rocks. His hair and beard were like drifts of snow. The birds had torn his belly open; it was a pit of raw meat, faintly steaming in the cold air.

The vultures hovered above. They were under attack. A goat, perched on a tablerock, was leaping straight up at the birds, trying to butt them in midair. The vultures swerved away, and the goat fell back on the rock, balancing itself perfectly on its hooves, ready for another leap. It was a black goat, a she-goat, the most beautiful animal Cadmus had ever seen. She was large as a stag, had ivory horns and ivory hooves, and eyes that were slits of yellow fire. But Cadmus did not stop to admire her. He had moved closer to the giant's snowy head.

"Hail, great Titan!" he said.

"Seeker, hail!"

"What did you call me, my lord?"

"Seeker."

"My name is Cadmus. Perhaps you think I'm someone else?"

"I think you're you; I speak to your condition, not your name. A seeker is one who seeks. You seek a sister. You seek a system. And you come to ask me how to find them."

"O wise one, you read my innermost hopes. The urgent task is to find my sister. Can you tell me of her?"

"She lives," replied the Titan. "She is unharmed."

"Where is she?"

"Out of your reach. In another mode."

"I don't understand," said Cadmus.

"She is lost to you. She has been placed beyond your grasp, or that of any other mortal."

"Then she is dead."

"She lives. There are those who would say that she has been magnified, glorified."

"Is she happy?"

"She is replete."

"Shall I see her again?"

"Only if you accomplish your task."

"And if I do, shall I?"

"When your task is done."

"What must I do first?"

"Begin," said Prometheus.

"Where?" asked Cadmus. "My eldest brother, Cyllix, who captains the war fleet of Phoenicia, has sailed westward with all his ships. My second brother, Phoenix, has marched his army eastward. But I, I have no fleet, no army. I am unfit to command, or even to serve in the ranks. I am alone, unarmed; which way do I go?"

"Your words reek of self-pity, my boy, which is no way to start a quest, or anything else. What has sapped your confi-

He was following a white fox; it
was scampering up the hill before him.

A naked giant was slung
between crags, chained to the rocks.

dence? Do people esteem your brothers over yourself? And do you share this opinion?"

"I do, I do. I envy my brothers—their raw animal magnetism, their meaty force."

"Do you really envy that single-minded ferocity, their gluttonous satisfaction in breaking an enemy's body in their own hands?"

"I have been taught that this is a royal aptitude," Cadmus said. "Lacking it, I cannot lead other men or win their respect. I simply have no impact on men or events. I think people only half hear me, half see me."

"Perhaps I detect something in you that your brothers lack," said Prometheus. "Something that can generate a force beyond crude muscular strength. However, that hidden talent must remain hidden if you continue to consult your doubts."

"I have dreamed of glory," said Cadmus. "Of mighty blows taken without flinching and mightier blows returned. Of foes falling, men shouting, women smiling. I have dreamed of slaying my sister's abductor. But such dreams are the wrack of a weakling's sleep. Real warriors sleep like hogs and dream with their swords."

"You are bitter for one so young. But such bitterness can become a strength if it is cleansed of self-pity. I have chosen you, Cadmus, but you must endorse my choice."

Cadmus didn't hear these last words. He had never before been where it was cold enough to make breath visible, and the puffs of white vapor coming out of the Titan's mouth as he spoke fascinated him. He was so deep in his reverie that he didn't catch the meaning of what was said.

"Why, I can *see* the words coming out of his mouth," he was saying to himself. "Just what I always wanted—to *see* sound and make others see it. Now I wonder if that steam is making different shapes for different sounds? No . . . this needs further study."

"Did you hear me?" boomed Prometheus, so loudly that he startled Cadmus out of his thoughts.

But the boy was used to hearing this from his father. "I just missed the last few words, my lord. The birds were screaming."

"You had better listen closely," said Prometheus. "I was saying that you must focus on what you can do, not what you can't."

"Well, I know what I *must* do. I must search for my sister. Somehow, I know that my brothers, for all their splendid virtues, won't find her."

"Neither will you, not yet. Why don't you ask me about your other quest?"

"What other?"

"Your quest for the magic code, for the word-signs."

"All that will have to wait."

"Two quests, yes, but you are one person, and your quests will merge. One will serve the other. Cadmus, Prince of the East, hearken to me. For all your diminutive stature and shrunken self-esteem, you are being ripened for mighty deeds."

"Again I ask: Where do I start?"

"You have already started. Go forth from this place. Ask questions. Cleave your way among the swarms of the indifferent, and the actively evil, and the few of accidental good will. A quest is not only a search; it is also a route that forms itself as it goes, striking a vein through circumstance. Go, Cadmus. Ask questions, test the answers, look, see, and understand so that wisdom and experience may irradiate the legacy you will leave mankind."

"What legacy?"

"I, Prometheus, gave the human race its first great gift—fire. You, Cadmus, shall give humanity the second great gift—a magic code to catch language on the wind and utter it anew for those who have learned the code. You have already begun with Aleph and Bet, the Ox and the House, and you shall go on to find a picture for every sound. That will be your gift."

"But you are being punished for your gift," said Cadmus. "Shall I be punished for mine?"

"In a different way, if you succeed. But they will try their best to see that you fail."

"Who are *they*?"

"They will make themselves known. They will send a dragon."

"After me?"

"None other."

"And what shall I do?"

"Fight him, of course."

"Fight a dragon? Me?!"

"You will not be alone. The black goat will go with you. She's no ordinary beast. She was born to Amalthea, the she-goat who was foster mother to the infant Zeus. Zeus became jealous

*It was a black goat . . . the most
beautiful animal Cadmus had ever seen.*

when this kid was born, and he tried to kill her. Therefore, does she hate Zeus, and now that she is grown, attempts to help me, whom Zeus considers his enemy."

"She's splendid, I can see that," said Cadmus. "But how can she help me against a dragon? I'm terrified at the very thought."

"Forget about fear. Look at those vultures up there, waiting until I'm alone so that they may feed again upon my liver; look at those cruel birds, my lad, and tell me you can't endure what must be endured."

"The spectacle of your suffering makes me ashamed of my cowardice. Yet, I'm still afraid."

*Cadmus turned and walked away down
the path. . . . The goat cast a last blazing
look at the birds above and trotted after him.*

"My dear boy, anyone who doesn't fear a dragon is a fool. But fight him you must, fear or not. When you leave here, you will make your way to the Great Smithy. There you must try to persuade Hephaestus to give you the weapons you'll need."

"How do I find the Great Smithy?"

"The goat knows the way."

"Master, I obey. I don't really know what I'm doing, but I know that I must do it."

"Go then, and my blessing go with you."

Cadmus touched the giant's beard timidly, then turned and walked away down the path. The goat cast a last blazing look at the birds above and trotted after Cadmus.

As soon as the goat left her rock, the vultures dived, their screams mingling with the Titan's groans. But Cadmus didn't notice. He was thinking too hard.

"I wonder whether breathing becomes more visible the colder it gets? Do different sounds freeze into different shapes? I'll have to go where it's really cold—behind the North Wind. When I have time perhaps—after the dragon and Europa and so forth. *Is* there any 'after' when meeting a dragon? Maybe I'd better do what I want first; save the monster and sister till later? Would that be ignoble? Am I heartless? Is my father right about me? Or is Prometheus?"

Something nudged him hard. He whirled about. The goat was looking at him with her yellow eyes. He stroked the harsh wool of her neck. She knelt and he mounted her. He held her horns as she trotted off. The wind smelled of snow and pine.

"I'm setting off on an awful journey, by any calculations," he said to himself. "Why then am I so happy?"

7

The Spider

The little lizard had returned to the palace in Eleusis and was now perched upon the beam over the royal bed, the very same spot from which he had watched his father die.

"The new king sleeps here now," Abas said to himself. "I shall wait until nightfall, and when he is deep asleep shall simply drop upon his exposed throat and sink my teeth into it. I know where the great vein is that runs from heart to brain. Yes. I shall drain his body of its lifeblood. I need the taste of it to cool my rage. But many hours must pass before nightfall, and the thought of killing him has sharpened my appetite. I think I'll do a bit of hunting."

Creeping along the beam, he came upon a spiderweb whose strands were much thicker than usual, but he was so excited by the memory of the dragon and the idea of becoming one himself—and of killing his brother that night—that he ignored what he knew: that a big, thick web means an outsize spider, one big enough to eat a lizard, perhaps.

Catching sight of a moth caught in the strands, Abas climbed onto the web and was pleased to find that it was strong enough to hold him.

Spider (1887) by Odilon Redon

But nothing moves faster than a spider in its web. This spider appeared so suddenly it was as if a piece of the web itself had clotted and come alive. Abas found himself confronting not the moth, but a spider bigger than any he had ever seen. To the little lizard it looked as big as a chariot wheel. In fact, it was about as big as a dinner plate.

Between two flicks of his tongue, the spider had already cast a loop of silk about him and pulled it tight, then cast another. Abas couldn't move. The spider pulled him closer and looked down at him with her multi-paned eyes. She spoke in a rustling voice.

"Were you about to steal my moth?"

"I beg your pardon," said Abas. "I thought this web was vacant. That you had gone off somewhere and that it didn't matter if I trespassed."

"Gone off, and left the larder full? You know more about spiders than that. I know you do, little thief. You've been robbing webs for a long time."

"Are you going to eat me?"

"You would certainly represent a change in diet," said the spider. "Actually you look quite edible under all that leather."

"How is it you speak so well?" asked Abas, stalling for time. He had puffed himself out when she cast the loops about him and was now slowly letting his breath out, trying to shrink away from her grasp. He was trying to keep the conversation going until he could manage to slip out of her loops. "Your command of the language is not only fluent, it's eloquent."

"You're pretty articulate yourself for a miserable little gecko," said the spider. "I speak for the same reason you do. I was not always a spider, as you were not always a lizard. Oh, my goodness, you're not trying to get away, are you? When we're conversing so nicely? That's not polite."

Swiftly, she cast three more loops about him, and drew them very tight. "If you're going to eat me, eat me now," cried Abas. "Get it over with!"

"I was once a maiden in the land of Lydia. . . .
Perhaps the most skillful spinner and weaver
amongst mortals since the world began."

"Gently, little friend," replied the spider. "Don't you want to hear my tale? Well, you will, whether you want to or not. You're a captive audience, you know."

"Yes, I know," murmured the lizard.

"I was once a maiden in the land of Lydia," said the spider. "Perhaps the most skillful spinner and weaver amongst mortals since the world began. I made garments that were lighter than silk but warmer than fur. And when I wove counterpanes, each square became a picture of some happy hour, making a quilt of joyous dreams. Well, I was on the threshold of a good life, anyone might think. I was honored in the countryside, well paid for my work, and several young men were eager to marry me. But, I made a fatal error. Carried away by pride, I boasted one day that I could spin and weave better than the goddess Athena."

"Are you Arachne, by any chance?" asked the lizard.

"By an evil chance, yes. I am Arachne."

"I've heard of you. Every child in the Middle Sea basin has heard nursery tales of you. How Athena grew angry at your boast and challenged you to a contest, which she won. And, as the price of losing, you were changed into a spider. You are the first of all spiders, mother of spiders."

"Is that what children are told?" asked Arachne.

"That's what I was told. Isn't it true?"

"Up to a point. Then it becomes a lie. Athena was indeed angered when she heard my boast. But she fell into a more murderous fury *after* the contest, which *I* won."

"You won?"

43

"I certainly did. And she had a big head start, you know. She set up her loom on top of a mountain. She didn't need a spindle; she didn't have to draw thread from flax. All she had to do up there was gather handfuls of cloud-wool and dye them in the colors of sunset and the colors of dawn. Then she wove the stuff on her loom and flung great colored tapestries across the sky. Oh, they were beautiful, all right. And the people stopped to look up and admire them. Then they hurried on their way to my door where the whole countryside had queued up, eagerly waiting for the cloaks and tunics and quilts that I was turning out so fast that I had clothed an entire village before Athena had flung out her first tapestry. The people were so happy they danced for joy in the meadow where my cottage stood, for it was threatening to be a hard winter. Oh, I won all right. And Athena knew it. She came striding down the mountain and stood there, taller than my cottage. She spoke in a voice that rattled the eaves:

" 'Stand forth, Arachne! Receive your award.'

"I came out and knelt before her. She glared down at me. Her gray eyes were like marsh water when the first scum of ice forms. She spoke again:

" 'Since you spin so well, and are so happy doing it, hereafter you shall be relieved of all other duties and can spend your life doing what you do best. Nor shall you need to concern yourself with heavy equipment—with spindle and distaff and loom. Out of your own body shall you draw all that you need.'

"I was dwindling as she spoke—shrinking, sprouting legs, antennae, becoming what you see before you now. When she had finished speaking I hung by a thread from my own lintel and was spinning a web.

" 'Yes,' she said. 'Spin, my friend, spin.'

> Spread your web
> so light and fine
> for that upon
> which you will dine.

"With those words, she took up my spindle and struck my loom, knocking it to splinters. Then she broke the spindle over her knee, and strode off. From then on, I was a spider."

"Have you lived here all this time, in the rafters of this palace?" asked the lizard.

"Not at all," said the spider. "I just arrived."

"And to what do we owe the honor of this visit, ma'am?"

"I was sent here—for you."

"For me? Who sent you?"

"Clotho, Lachesis, and Atropos. Did you not hear of them in your nursery tales?"

"Since you spin so well," said Athena, "you can spend your life doing what you do best."

"Have you lived here all this time, in the rafters of this palace?" asked the lizard.

"No ma'am. I don't think so."

"You should have. Some consider them more important than the gods themselves. They are the three crones who call themselves the Fates, and claim that they control destiny."

"Do they?"

"Who can tell? Everyone's afraid of them, so they probably do. They live in a hovel on a crag beyond Mount Olympus. There they sit, gnawing at pork bones and crusts of wheaten loaves, and swigging barley beer by the pail—and working as they eat. For they never stop doing either, except to sleep. And they don't sleep much. The youngest sister, Clotho, sits with comb and spindle, carding the flax and drawing the thread. The second sister, Lachesis, holds her notched rod, measuring out the thread. And the eldest sister, the most fatal crone, Atropos, the Scissors Hag, wields her shears, deciding where to cut the thread of each life—deciding, in other words, who lives and who dies. Then at midnight they leave their seats and go into a wild coven dance, tangling the threads, and calling the tangle a design. They have two pets, a cat and a spider. I am the spider. I was the first of my kind, and they liked my style and took me to live with them. The cat is my enemy, of course, but he can't catch me, no matter how he tries."

"Very interesting," said Abas. "But what, pray, do they want with me?"

"I have no idea," said the spider. "But they have decided, apparently, that you will play some role in the Master Design. So they have sent me for you, and where they send me, I go. What they bid me, I do. Come along then. I'll wrap you up just a bit more so you won't fall, and carry you there. We'll travel faster that way."

8

The Three Fates

achesis, the second Fate, held the little lizard on her lap and stroked his polished head with her forefinger.

"Atropos," she said, "the cat belongs to you. And Clotho, you have the spider. Neither loves me best, you have to admit. So I'm claiming this lizard for my own."

"He won't be staying with us," said Atropos. "He's here to receive instruction. Then out into the world he goes to play his role in our Master Design. You know that."

"But he's here now!" cried Lachesis. "And he's mine! And later, when he's out in the world, doing what he must do, perhaps he'll remember me now and then, and even visit me sometimes."

"Very well," said Atropos. "If you mean to adopt him you must be the one to instruct him."

"Oh, lizard mine," said Lachesis. "When you leave us you will go down the mountain, then eastward into the forest. You will search until you find a grove where the oaks grow to giant size. The birds there are larger too, and the insects. For there, buried deep, abides a fragment of the body of Uranus, the First One, the Rain God, butchered by his son Cronos at the dawn of time. The taproots of the trees in this place have drunk of his rich blood and grown large. And insects that eat the buds off the branches grow huge. The birds eat the insects, and wrens become as big as owls. But most wonderful of all, a greedy swarm of worms ate of the flesh, drank the blood of the butchered god, and grew enormous. They were filled with the boiling spite of that vengeful blood and put on armor, leather armor; they grew teeth, claws, and vicious spiked tails. And taught themselves the deadly trick of spitting fire.

"Now, my little green beauty," continued Lachesis, "you shall dig yourself a tunnel and burrow your way to the shoulder bone of Uranus. You shall eat your fill, and become a dragon also—a king among dragons, much larger than the ordinary kind, as you are now larger than a worm."

"I shall do all that you bid me, madam, and I thank you and your sisters for this your instruction. To become a dragon has been my fondest hope."

"It won't be all basking in the sun and gobbling cattle," said Atropos. "There are difficult tasks before you, risky ones, bloody ones."

"But that's what dragons are for!" cried Abas. "The opportunity to rend, crunch, destroy. Exactly why I have wanted to be one. Know this, venerable dame, there is a rage festering inside me that can be laved only by rivers of human blood."

"After you sharpen your skills on a few minor heroes," said Atropos, "and wipe out a village or two, you will go to Boeotia and await the coming of one Cadmus, a prince of Phoenicia. And that is your prime mission, to destroy him, leaving not a trace, not a morsel of flesh nor splinter of bone."

"Cadmus," said the lizard. "A great warrior?"

"Worse, much worse," said Atropos. "He's a meddler, a disciple of Prometheus. A mischief among mortals. One who views our mighty edicts as idle whim, who regards the Master Design as a web of cruel fantasy, and believes only in his own dreams—which he refuses to forget upon awaking, but pursues

all day long, trying to make them come true. The dream he pursues now is to steal a divine privilege and extend it to mankind."

"What privilege?" asked the lizard.

"It's called 'writing.'"

"What's that?"

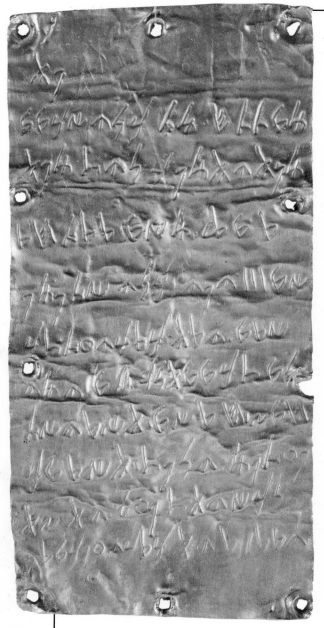

"It's what appears on the
Great Scroll. . . . It is a code,
a set of magic signs through which
language remembers itself
and utters itself anew.

"It's what appears on the Great Scroll. Only the gods know of it and understand its meaning. It is a code, a set of magic signs through which language remembers itself and utters itself anew. It will focus vague images and make them sing. It will make dreams dance. It can put wings to thought so that it passes from mind to mind, gaining strength as it goes, enriching the minds it touches and drawing forth those dangerous things called 'ideas,' which, if allowed to grow wild, will cause men and women to think they're as good as we are. In their pride, they will storm Olympus, hurl us off the mountain, and try to rule their own lives."

"And it is Cadmus who has set all this foul business afoot?" asked Abas.

"He and he alone. Although, if allowed to continue unchecked, he will certainly attract disciples. So he must be killed before he infects others. And the perfect antidote to the poison of ideas is a dragon."

"I am proud to have been chosen," said the lizard.

"Listen, little pet," said Lachesis. "You will have to practice on the standard warrior-brand of hero before tackling Cadmus. So I want you to heed this: Never eat a hero without peeling him. Make sure to spit out helmet, breastplate, greaves, sword, battle-ax—every last bit of indigestible gear. Otherwise, you'll get a monstrous bellyache. Do you promise?"

"I promise," said the lizard.

9

The Smith God

Mount Aetna, an extinct volcano in Sicily, was where Hephaestus had set up his first smithy. But Aetna suddenly decided to stop being extinct, and began to belch fire and spit red-hot lava. So the smith god moved forge and anvil to another dead crater in the eastern range of the Hellenic peninsula. And that is where the great black goat carried Cadmus.

The young prince dismounted and began to descend into the crater. He moved very cautiously. The place was full of sooty shadows. He winced at the great clamor rising from below. Metal struck metal, clanging and screeching. Rock rumbled. He heard ferocious laughter and shouting, cries of anger and pain. The noise was unbearable and the heat was worse. Cadmus felt as if he were standing right at the mouth of an open furnace.

Indeed, the huge figures he saw near the furnace pits wore thick leather aprons and helmets of hollowed rock with a single eyehole—one eyehole each in the middle of the forehead. And he knew that he was viewing creatures he had thought belonged only to legend—the Cyclopes, tall as trees, savage-tempered, master craftsmen who served the gods by laboring in the Great Smithy.

"What do you want?" boomed a voice. "Visitors are unwelcome here."

Swiftly, Cadmus tried to recover his wits, which had been scattered by the clamor and the heat. He knelt on the rock floor, for he recognized Hephaestus. The smith god was so huge that he seemed to fill the great crater. His enormous span of shoulders and broad chest were knotted with muscle. He wore a leather apron and swung the heaviest hammer ever made. Its shaft was the trunk of a tree, its head a single lump of iron larger than a boulder.

"Who are you?" the god roared.

Cadmus tried to answer but couldn't hear himself through the hammering and clanging. He jumped up on an anvil and spoke into the god's ear.

"O Hephaestus, mighty lord of mechanics and inventors, forgive my intrusion, but I have been sent to ask a favor."

"Who are you and what do you want? Be brief."

"I am Cadmus, a prince of Phoenicia, and am pledged to slay the Dragon of Boeotia."

"Presumptuous runt! How can you slay a dragon that has fattened itself on a diet of heroes?"

"Perhaps he has grown too fat," said Cadmus. "Perhaps he has been spoiled by heroes. Perhaps he has never met a clever coward. Perhaps the desperate strategies of sheer funk may prevail where heroics falter."

"Don't jest with me, little one," warned the god. "How can you possibly hope to slay a dragon?"

"With the weapons you will provide."

"As yet I have heard no reason I should do anything for you."

"My lord, I know that others come here loaded with treasure to repay you for what you alone can provide. But I, I can offer only my need, and can repay you only with gratitude."

"You're a persistent little fellow, I'll grant you that—and not uncourageous in your own way. Well, I happen to have some battle gear made for one who was killed before he could get here. A helmet of beaten brass which no battle-ax can dent. And a shield of brass, which no spear or sword can pierce. It is polished more brightly than any mirror so that you can flash the sun in your enemy's eyes. These weapons are for defense, but to conquer you must attack. Here is a sword of thrice-tempered iron that can cut through armor as easily as a tailor's shears slice through a bolt of wool. Watch this."

Hephaestus swung the sword and struck the anvil, splitting it cleanly in two.

Cadmus gawked at the gifts. The helmet was bigger than the great cooking pot used in the kitchen of his father's palace.

'I happen to have some battle gear. . . . A helmet of beaten brass which no battle-ax can dent.'

The shield was as big as a chariot wheel. And the sword . . . with its point stuck in the ground, Cadmus had to reach as high as he could to grasp its hilt.

"Don't you have something more my size?" he asked.

Hephaestus scowled. "This is the Great Smithy, you know. We forge weapons for gods and demigods and the larger heroes. Why don't you take your business to some village smith out there. I'm sure he'll be able to accommodate you."

"I can do without a helmet," murmured Cadmus. "Even one that fits would give me a headache. And the dagger you made for this same warrior will do me as a sword. And a single scale of that mail coat will make a fine shield; all it needs is a handle."

Hephaestus looked away. His face knotted in fury.

"I know how you must hate to alter your superb handi-work," said Cadmus. "But weapons are meant to be used; otherwise they are idle shapes of metal. And these are too big for me to use. Nevertheless, having seen them, I shall never be content with anything less splendid. Give me the dagger, I pray. And fix a grip for that brass disk. For I will not go from here weaponless. If you do not think me worthy to bear your arms, then be good enough to pitch me straightaway into your furnace flames so that my worthless carcass may help to fuel your mighty labors."

"A generous offer, but my fires require heartier fare. See."

Hephaestus was pointing at a Cyclops who held an enormous uprooted tree in each hand; he flung them into the flames.

"That's not the furnace," said Hephaestus. "Just a small fire for making charcoal. There's how they feed my forge-fires."

He was pointing to a pile of charcoal lumps that towered to the roof of the great cave. A line of Cyclopes stretched from that pile to a fire pit near an anvil as large as a courtyard. Buckets of charcoal were being passed from hand to hand. The Cyclops nearest the blaze tossed the black lumps in, whirled, and hurled the bucket over the heads of the others to the Cyclops at the charcoal pile. Each bucket was the size of a gardener's shed.

"No," murmured Cadmus. "I can see I'm not even worthy to feed your flames. I shall trouble you no more. Farewell."

"You have offered your all," said Hephaestus. "That's enough for me. Here's your dagger. And here's your shield. I have fixed a handle to it. Take them. Use them well. But you must have a helmet too. I insist. I'm the armorer; I know best. Take this brass thimble. I had intended it for Clotho, youngest of the Fates, but I'll make another for that dire spinster."

He clapped the thimble on Cadmus's head. It fit perfectly.

"If that tiny weight hurts your head, just think how it would ache under a touch of the dragon's claws," said Hephaestus.

Cadmus seized the smith god's great, grimy hand and kissed it. "Thank you, my lord. Memory of your kindness will lighten the heaviest gear. I shall bear your weapons with pride as great as the mightiest warrior can know."

"I must warn you," said Hephaestus, "that the gifts of the gods are not always what they seem. We extract heavy payment for what we give. It's our nature. This sword, for example; if it slays one of your enemies, it will insist on tasting the blood of one you love. I tell you this so that you may refuse the gift while you still have a chance."

Cadmus thought hard. The god's words terrified him, the more because they had been said with such kindness. "But there's no one I love except my sister," he said to himself. "And I have been told that a long time must pass before I see her again. Surely by then I shall have thrown the sword away. She'll be in no danger from me."

Aloud, he said: "Great Hephaestus, God of Fire, Master of Metal, I thank you for both weapons and warning. I shall keep your gifts and try to use them well."

"You're welcome, little one. Good hunting."

Cadmus climbed out of the crater and whistled for the goat. His new weapons were heavy, but they glittered so brightly, and the mountain air was so clean after the smoky forge that he grew half drunk on it and danced for joy. The goat pranced up to meet him. Cadmus flung his arms about her neck and rubbed her face with his. She bit his shoulder gently, then knelt while he climbed on her back. And down the slope of the great crater they went.

10

A New Dragon

bas obeyed those haggish sisters called the Fates and journeyed to an oak grove in the land of Boeotia where the shoulder bone of the butchered god had been buried. There the taproots of the trees had drunk of his rich blood and grown huge. The insects had eaten of the buds of these trees and grown huge. Birds had eaten the insects and grown enormous. And, deep underground, worms had feasted and grown into dragons.

When Abas reached the grove, he burrowed deep, as he had been told, and found the shoulder bone of Uranus. He ate of its magically replenished flesh and grew into a dragon. He was larger than any other dragon, with brass scales instead of leather ones, and brass claws. His tail had spikes of iron instead of bone. His breath was now aflame, not only with his own spite, but with that of the ancient god whose scattered body still called for vengeance.

Abas came into that grove a little lizard; he came out as an enormous dragon. Full of bloodthirsty zeal, he immediately began to terrorize the countryside. He devoured cattle, cowherds, sheep, shepherds—and wiped out entire villages. Throughout the land, he became known as the Dragon of Boeotia, or Abas the Abominable.

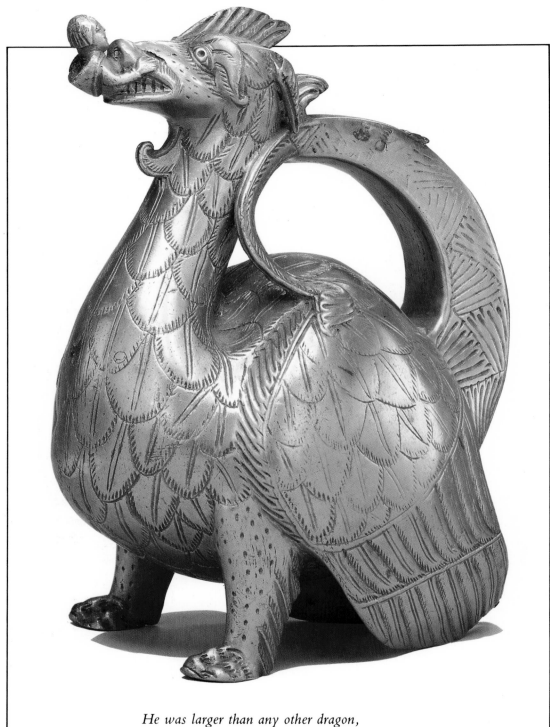

He was larger than any other dragon,
with brass scales instead of leather ones.

One other thing happened to this dragon who had been a lizard, and before that, a prince. Having taken a monster form, and behaving as a monster, his human brain had clenched, shriveled and become reptilian. Stupefied by successful cruelty, he was losing the power to reason, and was quite happy without it.

11

Journey to Boeotia

From the Great Smithy to Boeotia was a long overland journey. Cadmus had no idea where Boeotia might be, and in those days travelers did not stop to ask directions. It was too dangerous. For the savagely inhospitable tribesmen along the route were very likely to offer strangers as sacrifice. In that region, sacrifice was made to a bat goddess, who would refuse to bless the orchards without her ration of human blood.

So Cadmus did not stop to ask his way but let the goat take him where she would. He knew that she was under some mandate from Prometheus and was guided by secret knowledge. And he was in no hurry to reach the hunting grounds of the dragon.

Prince and goat were traveling northward now along the shore of a narrow gulf. Across the bay, mountains loomed. But on their shore were flatlands. They came to a place where the gulf opened into what seemed to be a river.

The goat waded in and began to drink, then moved upstream and dipped her muzzle again. Cadmus tasted the water too, and realized that the salt gulf was turning to brackish river water. It was almost sunset, an early dusk because of the mountains to the west. The river, bathed in red light, looked like blood flowing from some great wound in the earth. Cadmus shuddered. He was seized by a premonition of evil. Suddenly, he knew what he had to do, although it would almost break his heart to do it.

"I must leave you here," Cadmus told the goat. "I shall strike inland, following this river. I understand that dragons and such favor the banks of freshwater streams; they find good hunting where man and beast come down to drink. You wait here for me. Wait seven days. I shall return when I have killed the dragon. If I don't return, farewell to you."

The goat nodded. She had no intention of obeying, but was glad that Cadmus had chosen this route. Now she could follow the river, keeping out of sight, but knowing all the time that he was just ahead. For she intended to be there when he met the dragon.

Cadmus followed the river upstream all day, and grew to dislike it. He was used to the swift, tumbling little rivers of the foothills near his home. This one cut through flatlands, was broad and shallow, and seemed to have no current. It oozed rather than flowed. A green scum flecked its surface. He would have preferred to angle away toward the forest. But some instinct told him to stay near the slow river.

He slept on its bank that night. A brown mist arose and thickened into a tall shape. A voice grated down at him: "I am Asopus, an ancient river god. The high thief, Zeus, stole my daughter, the beautiful naiad Aegina. When I protested, he pelted me with boulders, wounding me to death but never allowing me to die. So that I flow forever in a pestilential stream and am loathed by man because a dragon now harries my shores and litters them with corpses, making my waters fouler still. Nor shall I be cleansed until the dragon is killed."

"I have come to kill it. Tell me where to find it, O river god, that I may cleanse your waters."

"I do not know where the dragon is," said Asopus. "I break into many streams at this point. For this is where Zeus broke my body with boulders."

"Can't you give me any idea where to find the monster?" asked Cadmus.

Follow a cow
She'll show you how.

The grating voice dwindled away. The mist cleared. Cadmus moaned and fell into a deeper sleep. When he awoke he saw a cow grazing nearby. She lifted her head, lowered it again to wrench out another mouthful of grass, and then ambled over to the youth. She was a pretty brown heifer with large amber eyes

"I flow forever in a pestilential stream,
and am loathed by man because a dragon
now harries my shores and litters them with corpses."

April Mood (1946/55) by Charles Burchfield

When Cadmus awoke he saw a cow grazing nearby.

and small horns. She mooed musically, then moved off. Cadmus followed. He understood nothing. He knew only that he must do as the river god had bidden him.

For the rest of that day Cadmus followed the cow. She kept to the shore of a stream that branched northwest. Her ambling pace was swifter than it looked, and Cadmus found it hard to keep up. He could not stop to eat or drink. Night came. Surely, Cadmus thought, she'll rest now. But she did not. The stars hung low and it was still easy to see her.

The heifer climbed a low hill and went down the other side. Cadmus followed. His legs were weary. The shield and sword seemed to weigh more with every step. They dragged him toward the ground. "Heavy, heavy, these gifts of the gods," he murmured. "But if their favor is such a burden, how weighty must be their displeasure." He stumbled on. He could not cast off his weapons, nor could he rest while the heifer moved forward.

All night Cadmus followed her. His legs turned to bladders. He staggered and sank to the ground.

"Am I to fail before I even reach the dragon? Simply because I am weary? No! This shall not be."

He pulled himself to his hands and knees but could rise no farther. The cow was moving out of sight. He crawled after her. He tried to encourage himself by thinking that she too was tiring. She was climbing the steep slope of another hill. Cadmus struggled up the hill, dragging himself along on his knees, pulling himself by the strength of his arms. Finally, the cow reached the top of the hill and began to go down the other side. Now Cadmus simply let himself roll. When she started across the plain, he again crawled after her. His hands were scraped, his knees, bleeding. He could see the river glinting in the afternoon sun, and realized they had worked their way back to the main branch.

"I will go on even if my flesh is torn away and I have to creep on my bones," he said to himself.

Then, to his delight, he saw the cow suddenly fold herself into a low shadow and lie down. As he watched, she lowered her head and slept. Cadmus drew in a deep breath of fresh air. He took off his helmet, laid down his shield, and placed his sword carefully upon it. His eyelids sagged, but he kept them open a moment to savor the marvelous idea that he could close them when he wished, and sleep.

To his horror he saw the cow's shadow grow tall again as she arose and moved on. He tried to get up but was nailed to the ground. Groaning, he took his sword, stuck it in the ground, and then, holding the hilt, dragged himself up. He clapped the helmet on his aching head, then took a great breath, and lifted his shield. He couldn't hold it but had to drag it behind him as he limped after the cow. He knew he couldn't walk far. He knew also that he dared not sink to his knees again and crawl because his legs were raw meat now. He would never be able to bear the pain of crawling over the rocky ground.

The moon had risen. The stars flared. The meadow was flooded with brown light. Now the cow seemed to be walking on her hind legs. He blinked and looked again. The cow danced before him, shaking one raised forehoof at the moon.

That sight finished him. Sword and shield slipped from his grasp and fell clanking. He dropped to the ground. His helmet rolled away. He lay on his back looking at the moon. It was a curdled yellow that seemed to pulse in the sky as he watched. His throat was so dry that he couldn't swallow. He moved his

The stars flared. The meadow
was flooded with brown light.

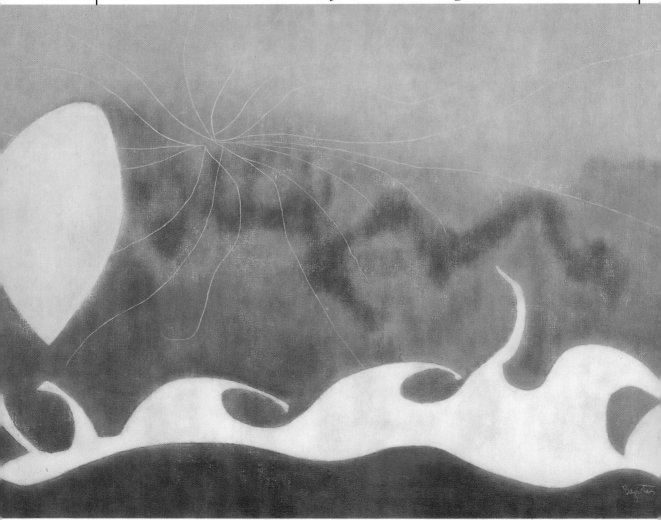

The Beach (1955) by William Baziotes

tongue but could work up no spittle. He had not eaten all day, but thirst made him ignore his hunger. His thirst was unbearable, but he hadn't the strength to drag himself across the field to the river.

Cadmus swiveled his neck painfully to look at the cow. If she had been dancing, she had stopped. She was cropping grass again. He tried to call to her, heard himself croaking feebly. He gathered up the last tatters of his strength and sent a thought toward her. "Come here!" She raised her head, swung her tail, and loped toward him. Her swollen bag swung above him. He grasped it, pulled himself up, and tried to drink from her udder.

The cow pulled away. She was skittish. She was moving off. Cadmus fell back onto the grass. "If I don't drink, I'll die," he thought. He flung himself on his helmet and rolled to his knees. It was agony. He forced himself to bear the pain, and crawled toward the cow. He grasped her. She did not skitter. She stood. Cadmus milked her into his helmet. Twin jets tinkled in. The sound gave him strength enough to keep milking until the helmet was half full. He tried to lift it in both hands, but they were shaking so much that he had to put it down. He stretched himself on the ground and drank from the helmet like a snake out of a trough. Every swallow of the warm rich milk was the taste of life itself. He drank every drop. The cow had ambled off again, but stood closer than before, wrenching grass. His belly full, his thirst quenched, Cadmus didn't move, didn't want to. He felt deliciously drowsy and closed his eyes.

Screams woke him, terrible, hoarse, bellowing screams. The cow was screaming. Brass tinkled strangely. Great brass claws were digging into her. The moon was covered by clouds; it was hard to see. The cow was rising slowly into the air, bellowing horribly—a dreadful, clotted, phlegmy sound. Metal wings clanked. Cadmus smelled sulfur and dung. He saw a gout of red fire, and, by its light, a huge lizard shape. It disappeared into the blackness above, taking the cow with it.

12

Fighting the Dragon

Cadmus was dizzy with horror. He didn't know whether he was awake or asleep, but he feared he was awake. "It took the cow," he thought. "It'll be back for me." But he could not move. Fatigue was stronger than fear. He fell into a suffocated sleep.

The cow danced in his sleep. She frisked on hind legs and beckoned him with one forefoot, crying, "Moon! moon!" He arose and danced with her. One brisket was torn away; the raw meat bulged. But it did not sicken him; he pitied her too much. He danced with her in the moonlight—dim brown light; the moon swam in a chink of clouds; it was brown as an old bloodstain. The cow's eyes were pits of amber light; her white horns glistened. Her breath was heavy and sweet with the smell of cropped grass.

They danced down to the river. The moon flared, casting a yellow light, turning the river into a mirror. The cow gazed at herself in the water. Her head swayed. She mooed at her reflection.

In the clarity of his stunned, moonstruck sleep, Cadmus knew that this play of cow and mirrored cow held great meaning for him somehow, that this was why he had been commanded to follow her. But what the meaning was he did not know. The cow bellowed and disappeared.

Cadmus awoke at dawn. His weapons lay on the grass; the cow was gone. He looked about. He lay in a circle of trampled grass. He tried to remember what had happened. Suddenly, the air was filled with a hideous clanking sound. The sun was blotted by an enormous shadow. He smelled fire.

"It's here," he said to himself. "I'm about to die."

Shuddering, he looked up. It was worse than he had thought; it was the most dreadful sight imaginable. A crocodile as big as a ship, a flying crocodile with brass wings. The monster's hide was made of sliding brass scales; its long, thick tail bristled with iron spikes. Its feet wore brass claws. And, from its jaws, spurted hot, red fire.

The dragon was still a mile away, but Cadmus could feel the awful heat as he stood there on the plain. "Well," he said to himself. "I understand that the waters of the Styx are very cold. So my first sensation of death should be refreshing."

But he could not hearten himself. He almost swooned in the stinking blasts of heat. There was no way under the morning sun that he could fight this flaming spiked beast. Now the heat had become unbearable. Clutching sword and shield, with helmet firmly planted on his head, he rushed to the river.

All this time, the black goat had been following Cadmus, but she had found it no easy task. For the beasts of the forest, never having encountered a giant goat, considered anything with horns their natural prey. She had fought off a lion, goring it severely, but had herself been raked by its claws before it had slunk away. Then a pack of wolves had caught the scent of her blood and hunted her over the fields. She outran them eventually, but was forced to make a great circle back to the river. She had lost time, but had finally caught up with Cadmus. As she entered the meadow, she saw the dragon hovering and Cadmus diving into the river. She positioned herself on the shore as close as possible to where he had dived, keeping her hooves on a flat rock.

Cadmus had dived as deep as he could, holding his breath. The water grew warm as the dragon passed overhead, but the flames could not reach him. He waited, crouching on the bottom of the river until he heard the clanging fade. Then he kicked

The cow frisked on hind legs and beckoned
him with one forefoot, crying, "Moon! Moon!"

*All this time, the black
goat had been following Cadmus.*

against the bottom, heading for the surface. But he could not move. His weapons were too heavy.

He struggled. He could not surface. Iron bands tightened around his chest. Pain spiked him. He began to gag. One instant more and he would have to take a breath, even of water. He opened his right hand and let the shield go. Then he shot to the surface and floated there, panting. The dragon, wheeling above, saw him surface. It folded its brass wings like a giant pelican and plunged toward the water.

Down, down, straight at the floating Cadmus, hurtled the monster. The goat sprang up at the dragon, just as it had sprung at the vultures tormenting Prometheus. She hurled herself between monster and prey. The brass beast struck the goat with the full weight of its dive, breaking every bone in her body.

Cadmus was not aware that the goat had come. But he saw the dragon swerve suddenly and fly off carrying a dark mass in its claws. It dropped what it was carrying, rose high, flew a distance, but did not vanish. Cadmus threw his sword onto the bank. He dived down to the river bottom, found his shield, and hauled it to the surface. Then he climbed out and retrieved his sword. The dragon was a speck in the sky. It was growing larger.

Cadmus heard a hoarse moaning sound. He dropped his weapons and ran back to the riverbank. He fell to his knees and embraced the dying goat. He kissed her face, weeping, pleading, "Don't die. Please don't."

But the hard, graceful body was broken and bleeding, all power fled. She twitched piteously, moaning. Only her eyes were alive, golden, more sentient than ever. She looked at Cadmus, and he read the plea in her eyes. He arose, walked away, picked up his sword, and came slowly back.

He stooped beside her and gently closed her eyes; for he knew he could not do what he must do if they were open. Then he kissed her. "I'll see you in Hades," he said. He raised his sword over his head with both hands and struck down, point first. He stabbed through the body, driving a last sound out of it, and all tension. The body flopped loosely. The goat was dead.

Cadmus had forgotten about the dragon. Now he turned and looked up. He was ready to be killed. A notion half formed itself. He would drop his weapons, let the dragon strike as it would. Then his soul would join the goat's, and they would enter Hades together. He was slimy with mud, exhausted, sick of living, afraid of dying. But he did not drop his sword. Once again the cruel pattern had asserted itself—brutality assuming more power, more purpose than innocence and playfulness. Snuffing aspiration, nullifying questions, imposing a doomed certainty.

If only the pattern could be challenged at just one point it might alter the whole. If just once, he thought, size could be overcome by wit, foulness by fair intent.

The dragon was overhead, hovering. Cadmus, holding his sword, felt a nausea of fear. For all his fancy thoughts, he knew he was afraid of pain, afraid of dying, and terror held every priority.

"No wonder evil always wins," he said to himself. "We fatten it with our fear."

Cadmus looked up at the dragon. "What's it waiting for?" he asked himself. "Bigger game? A worthier foe? Look at it. It's only an oversized lizard after all, winged and armored, to be sure, and bristling with iron spikes and shooting fire. Still, this formidable apparatus is directed by a brain the size of a hazelnut. Or is it? It seems to be making a decision. Does it really find me too small to bother with? Do I hope so? Then why have I come all this way? I warned Prometheus I was miscast in this role. One needs to be a bit monstrous to vanquish monsters. I'm too light for this work, not ruthless enough. I have the impulse, though, I just lack the equipment.

"Still hovering. . . . If I possessed an ounce of heroism, I'd beat sword on shield until it dived. Heroes need dragons. Who needs heroes? Men do. And the gods need men for their entertainment. Yes, but this entertainment will fail. I warn you, gods, if evil continues to be so successful, success will lose its prestige. Losers will inherit your earth, and you'll grow so bored with them you'll send another flood."

A cleft of lightning stood weirdly on the blue sky. Cadmus heard thunder; it rumbled like the voice of Prometheus.

> To make the dragon yield,
> let him dread his head
> upon your shield.

*A cleft of lightning stood
weirdly on the sky. Cadmus
heard thunder . . . like the voice of Prometheus.*

Then silence. Cadmus tried to puzzle out the message. He knew it was of the utmost importance and that he did not have much time. He heard the brass scales clanking. The dragon was still directly overhead, wheeling. "These rhymes and riddles have

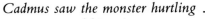
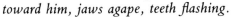

proved useful," he said to himself. "And I dare not ignore this one. But what does it mean? I have a shield, true enough, but what does it have to do with the dragon's head?"

Cadmus stared into the shield. It was a blur of brightness. He blinked. What he saw was his own face. "That's it!" he cried. "I understand! The dragon must see itself in my shield. But to do that, it will have to come very close, much too close. Bless me, Prometheus, for here it is!"

Indeed, a great shadow had darkened the plain. The hot breath of the beast was scorching the grass. Cadmus saw it, jaws yawning, swooping toward him in a long, curving dive. The dragon swept low and struck at Cadmus with one great brass claw. Brass rang on brass as claw struck helmet. But Cadmus was not hurt; the claw did not pierce the helmet. The dragon swerved in the air, flailing its spiked tail. Cadmus stood, sword lifted. "Keep your bargain, Hephaestus," he muttered. "I've paid in advance. The sword has killed the one I love. Let it now kill the one I hate."

He swung the blade and sliced off the tip of the dragon's tail. The beast howled in agony, rose to a great height, and came diving down again, furiously beating its wings and lashing its mutilated tail. He looked up and saw the monster hurtling toward him, jaws agape, teeth flashing. It was falling with tremendous force, but Cadmus stood his ground.

"Now's the time to test the rhyme," he thought. He held up the shield so that its bright disk covered his face and torso. He stood rooted to the ground. The dragon dove headfirst toward the polished brass disk and saw a terrible sight—its own reflection in the mirror of the shield. The beast had never seen itself before and did not know it was looking at itself, but thought another monster was attacking. When it spat flame at the shield, it saw the monster facing it spit flame right back. The dragon gasped in horror.

Now gasping in horror means drawing one's breath in. And that's exactly what the dragon did. It drew in a great draft, not of air, but of fire. It inhaled its own flame. Fire entered its body, burning everything inside. Lungs, liver, and heart were burned to a crisp.

With a choking shriek of agony the dragon fell to the scorched plain. The fire quickly worked itself outward, and, as Cadmus watched, the whole great length of the monster burned with a bright blue flame. The air was filled with bitter smoke. But the fumes were sweet to Cadmus. The fire finally subsided, leaving only a handful of brass scales and ivory teeth.

The dragon, in its last agony, had scorched and flattened the grass in a great circle.

"Thank you, Prometheus," cried Cadmus. "In your rhyme evil saw its face and choked on its own bile. And thank you again for choosing so unlikely a champion and holding to your choice. Thank you, Hephaestus, for sword and shield. The cost was heavy but no more than you warned. And thank you, thank you, beloved goat, for flinging yourself between me and the monster and taking the death that should have been mine."

He could say nothing more. He was wracked by loss. He wanted to weep, but could not. His sorrow was too deep for tears. He returned to the body of the goat. Not much was left;

Flowers sprang—beautiful, yellow and black flowers like the first spillings of sunlight on the grass.

the dragon's final fire had consumed it. He lifted a charred piece of skull and looked into the scorched eye sockets. Abrim with yellow light they had been, fierce with loyalty, smoldering with intelligence. They were charred pits now. Cadmus wept. Where she had lain and begged for death, he stood and wept.

His tears fell on the charred bones. Flowers sprang—beautiful yellow and black flowers like the first spillings of sunlight on the grass. They were a kind of daisy, a brave, hardy flower, bright and joyous, strong as weeds. We call them black-eyed susans.

Cadmus stood looking at them. He was weary, battered. He wanted to fling himself full length into that flower bed and sleep there forever. A breeze arose. The flowers swayed and murmured. The murmuring became words: "Do not rest," whispered the flowers. "Not yet . . ."

"Who are you who speak?" asked Cadmus. "My goat? The voice of madness? If so, let me be mad."

The flowers whispered again: "I die but shall live in a tale that will be told. Not just in song, but dwelling forever in your magic signs."

Then the breeze had fallen; the voices of the flowers had faded; they were almost too faint to hear. Their final words were

"Beware the dragon's teeth." But the sound was so faint that Cadmus heard it as "*Bury* the dragon's teeth."

It seemed an odd instruction, but Cadmus could not ignore the last words spoken by the flowers that had sprung from the body of his beloved goat. He stumbled to the heap of teeth and picked up a handful. With his sword he poked holes in the field, made even rows, and one by one buried the teeth as a gardener plants his seeds.

13

The Buried Teeth

hese seeds grew with monstrous speed. Spikes poked out of the ground. Then brass pots pushed out; they were not pots, but helmets. The helmets were on heads, and the heads on shoulders. Cadmus watched in wonder as full-size warriors burst from the soil, brushing clods of earth off their gear. The brass armor they wore had been corroded by the damp earth and seemed as green as dragon's hide.

The warriors stood in ranks, motionless. Cadmus realized that they were awaiting some word of command. But no one had emerged as their leader. Cadmus hated them at sight, and feared them. They had been spawned by the dragon, and he himself had been tricked into planting the seed from which they had sprung. How? Why? Was this another jape of the Fates? Must his victory contain defeat?

Cadmus had stepped behind a tree when the helmets had begun to appear so that he could not be seen. He picked up a rock and threw it. The rock struck a helmet. The warrior whirled about and smote the one standing next to him with the haft of his spear. The man who had been hit struck back. In a moment, the whole troop was fighting—striking, slashing, thrusting. Cad-

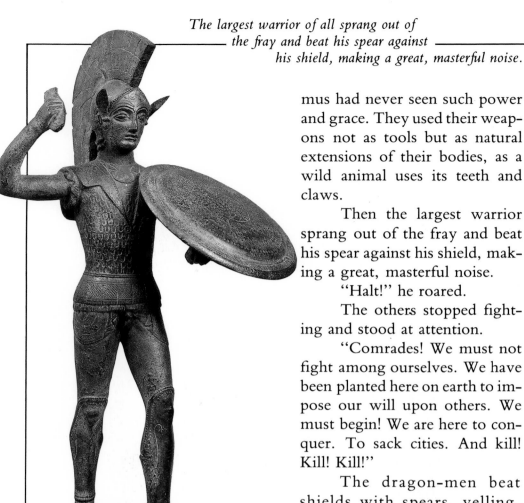

mus had never seen such power and grace. They used their weapons not as tools but as natural extensions of their bodies, as a wild animal uses its teeth and claws.

Then the largest warrior sprang out of the fray and beat his spear against his shield, making a great, masterful noise.

"Halt!" he roared.

The others stopped fighting and stood at attention.

"Comrades! We must not fight among ourselves. We have been planted here on earth to impose our will upon others. We must begin! We are here to conquer. To sack cities. And kill! Kill! Kill!"

The dragon-men beat shields with spears, yelling, "Kill! Kill! Kill!" Their faces shone with ferocious glee. Their leader raised his sword and rushed off. They rushed after him.

Dazed with horror, Cadmus had drifted out from behind his tree. One of the warriors spotted him. Without breaking stride, the soldier made a backhand swipe with his spear, pierced Cadmus's side, withdrew the spear all in one motion, and raced off.

The breeze had risen again. The flowers sighed, "Cadmus, Cadmus."

He felt a fever pulsing inside of him. He realized that he

must finish his magic code, but his strength was going fast. He scrabbled at the tree and peeled off a piece of bark. He dipped a twig into the blood of his wound, and began to draw.

Pictures flowed into his head—ordinary things, the closest things, things everyone knows. He drew them—water, fish, hand, mouth, field, fence, camel, door, hook. With his blood he drew simplified pictures of these things, each picture standing for the first sound of their names.

How many sounds were there? Did he have them all? The field was tilting. The trees were spinning. The flowers were silent. How many sounds? Twenty-two. He lacked one. Yes. *P-p-p-p.* What word began with that sound? He was puckering his mouth. That was it! Of course! *Pe,* "mouth." He drew a mouth.

Pictures flowed into his head — ordinary things, the closest things, things everyone knows. Cadmus drew them.

*When Demeter looked down and saw
Cadmus lying dead near the riverbank . . . she
decided to bless his labors and make them fruitful.*

The sounds were all scrambled. Someone else would have to straighten them out. But he had found them all, every one. Now he could rest, and search for the black goat in the Land Beyond Death. There too, he knew, he would finally find his sister Europa again.

His eyes closed. He had done what he had to do; he could die now.

Demeter, Goddess of the Harvest, fell into a rage when she learned that one of her fields had been used to grow a crop of dragon-men, spawned by the monster she herself had cursed. When she looked down and saw Cadmus lying dead near the riverbank, and learned that he had killed the dragon, she decided to bless his labors and make them fruitful.

She cast a healing spell upon the field. Where the blood of Cadmus had soaked into the earth, another crop grew, not of killers, but of clever, gentle creatures who roamed the lands of the Middle Sea basin, teaching the Cadmean alphabet. They were known as *Sileni*, the wood gods, and wherever they went they trapped language in their net of magic signs. They taught others to read and write so that the bitter lessons of history, the wisdom of Prometheus, and the beauty of the old songs were able to utter themselves anew.

And when people could read what wiser ones had said, it became more difficult for the dragon-men to prevail.

Acknowledgments

Letter Cap Illustrations by Hrana L. Janto

Opposite page 1, CERES, *Limoges enamel by Martial Reymond*
    Courtesy of The Frick Collection, New York

Page 2, CHRYSANTHEMUMS, *by Hokusai*
    Courtesy of the Musée Guimet, Paris
        Photo: Giraudon/Art Resource, New York

Page 4, FRUIT (WITH BUTTERFLY AND LIZARD), *by Rachel Ruysch (1664–1750)*
    Courtesy of the Uffizi, Florence
        Photo: Scala/Art Resource, New York

Page 6, PORTRAIT OF POET MENANDRO *from Pompeii, Casa del Menandro*
    Courtesy of Scala/Art Resource, New York

Page 8, THE ARTIST'S MOTHER, *by Albrecht Dürer (1471–1528)*
    Courtesy of Marburg/Art Resource, New York

Page 11, THE COURSE OF EMPIRE: DESTRUCTION, *by Thomas Cole (1801–1848)*
    Courtesy of The New-York Historical Society

Page 12, HERMES, *statue in pietra calcarea, Niveveh, Baghdad*
    Courtesy of Scala/Art Resource, New York

Page 14, SPREAD OF THOUGHT, *by Victor Brauner, 1956*
    Courtesy of The Solomon R. Guggenheim Museum, New York; Gift, Mr. and
    Mrs. Jean de Menil, 1958

Page 17, DOGE ANDREA GRITTI, *by Titian (1488/90–1576)*
    Courtesy of The National Gallery of Art, Washington, D.C.; Samuel H. Kress
    Collection

Page 18, RAPE OF EUROPA, *by Veronese (1370/74–1460)*
    Courtesy of Palazzo Ducale, Venice
        Photo: Alinari/Art Resource, New York

Page 20, MIMBRES LIZARD BOWL
   Courtesy of The Peabody Museum, Harvard University, 99-12-10/53221, neg. #T764

Page 22, AMBULACRO DELLA GRANDE CASSIA, *detail*
   Courtesy of Piazza Armerina
      Photo: Scala/Art Resource, New York

Page 23, THE POLISH RIDER, *by Rembrandt (1606–1669)*
   Courtesy of The Frick Collection, New York

Page 24, DECORAZIONE, *from Pompeii, Villa dei Misteri*
   Courtesy of Scala/Art Resource, New York

Page 26, THE PUNISHMENT OF PROMETHEUS, *by Anthony Van Dyck (1599–1641)*
   Courtesy of Douai, Musée de la Chartreuse
      Photo: Giraudon/Art Resource, New York

Page 28, MIMBRES BAT BOWL
   Courtesy of The Arizona State Museum, University of Arizona
      Photo: Helga Teiwes

Page 30, RAVINE, *oil painting by Vincent van Gogh (1853–1890)*
   Courtesy of The Museum of Fine Arts, Boston; Bequest of Kevin McLeod

Page 33, BLUE FOX, *by David True, 1986*
   Courtesy of private collection
      Photo: Blum-Hellmann Gallery, New York

Page 34, COPPA LACONICA CON SISFO E TITIO NELL'ADE
   Courtesy of the Vatican
      Photo: Scala/Art Resource, New York

Page 37, DEER, *from Niaux, France*
   Courtesy of Mazonwicz/Art Resource, New York

Page 38, PAESSAGGIO, *prov da Pompeii, Naples*
   Courtesy of the Museo Nazionale, Pompeii
      Photo: Scala/Art Resource, New York

Page 40, SPIDER, *by Odilon Redon (1840–1916)*
   Courtesy of The Museum of Modern Art, New York; Mrs. Bertram Smith Fund

Page 43, PENELOPE CHE TESSE, *by Stradana*
   Courtesy of Palazzo Vecchio, Sala di Penelope, Florence
      Photo: Scala/Art Resource, New York

Page 45, L'INDUSTRIA, *by Veronese*
   Courtesy of Palazzo Ducale, Venice
      Photo: Alinari/Art Resource, New York

Page 46, STUDY OF AN IGUANA, *by Charles Darwin from* On the Beagle
   Courtesy of Snark/Art Resource, New York

Page 48, LES SORCIERES, *after Fuseli*
   Courtesy of coll. Peral
      Photo: Snark/Art Resource, New York

Page 51, IN THE WOODS, *by Asher Durand (1796–1886)*
   Courtesy of The Metropolitan Museum of Art, New York; Gift in memory of Jonathan Sturges by his children, 1895

Page 52, LAMINA ARUEA DA PYRIGIA CON ISCRIZIONE II
   Courtesy of the Museo del Villa Giul, Rome
      Photo: Scala/Art Resource, New York

Page 54, ERUPTION OF VESUVIUS IN 1779, *by Volaire*
   Courtesy of the Musée des Beaux-Arts, Rouen
      Photo: Giraudon/Art Resource, New York

Page 56, THE BLACKSMITH, *by Ernst Ludwig Kirchner (1880–1938)*
   Courtesy of Marburg/Art Resource, New York

Page 57, ELMO D'ORO DA UR
   Courtesy of The Baghdad Museum
      Photo: Scala/Art Resource, New York

Page 60, GREEN DRAGON, *from Arthur Rackham's Book of Pictures, plate 23*
   Courtesy of The New York Public Library, Prints Collection

Page 62, FEATHERED TWO-FOOTED DRAGON, *late 12th–early 13th century*
   Courtesy of The Metropolitan Museum of Art, New York, The Cloisters Collection, 1947
      Photo: Lynthon Gardiner

Page 64, ARQUES-LA-BATAILLE, *by John H. Twachtman (1853–1902)*
   Courtesy of The Metropolitan Museum of Art, New York; Morris K. Jessup Fund, 1968

Page 67, AN APRIL MOOD, *by Charles Burchfield, 1946/55*
   Courtesy of The Collection of the Whitney Museum of American Art, New York, purchase, with funds from Mr. and Mrs. Lawrence A. Fleischman

Page 68, EVENING GLOW—THE OLD RED COW, *by Albert Pinkham Ryder (1847–1917)*
   Courtesy of The Brooklyn Museum, New York, 13.34, Frederick Loeser Fund

Page 70, THE BEACH, *by William Baziotes, 1955*
   Courtesy of The Whitney Museum of American Art, New York, purchase
      Photo: Geoffrey Clements

Page 72, THE YELLOW COW, *by Franz Marc (1880–1916)*
   Courtesy of The Solomon R. Guggenheim Museum, New York
      Photo: Carmelo Guadagno

Page 75, YOUTH LEADING SACRIFICIAL BULL, *from the Parthenon, north frieze*
   Courtesy of Athens Acropolis Museum
      Photo: Marburg/Art Resource, New York

Page 76, RAM IN A THICKET, *2600 B.C.*
   Courtesy of The University Museum, University of Pennsylvania

Page 79, THUNDERSTORM, *by Arthur G. Dove (1880–1946)*
   Courtesy of The Columbus Museum of Art

Page 80, GORGON
   Courtesy of the Delphi Museum
      Photo: Lukas/Art Resource, New York

Page 82, SUNFLOWER, *oil on canvas by Joan Mitchell, 1981*
   Courtesy of Christie's, New York

Page 84, EXECUTION SCENE, *from the Chronicle of Carrarienbus, Bib. Marciana*
   Courtesy of SEF/Art Resource, New York

BOOKS BY BERNARD EVSLIN

Merchants of Venus
Heroes, Gods and Monsters of the Greek Myths
Greeks Bearing Gifts: The Epics of Achilles and Ulysses
The Dolphin Rider
Gods, Demigods and Demons
The Green Hero
Heraclea
Signs & Wonders: Tales of the Old Testament
Hercules
Jason and the Argonauts

Tulsi is antimicrobial and anti-inflammatory. A strong compress made from fresh plant material is healing for cuts, scratches, and other minor abrasions. It's also mildly analgesic and can be added to your formulas for this purpose. A tincture is also a sensible way to use this herb topically. It's an excellent acne treatment and I combine pulverized tulsi leaves with aloe to make a soothing face mask. As we discussed earlier, tulsi serves well as an insect repellent (see page 41).

In the Kitchen

I love to add ribbons of fresh tulsi to stir-fries. I just toss a small handful of the leaves into the pan, along with garlic, cayenne pepper, and some olive oil, to build an aromatic base before adding the meats and vegetables. I enjoy the flavor of this herb with chicken or fish, but it's also quite good with pork. In a pork dish, I also add some grated fresh ginger as well as some fine slices of lemon balm to round out the flavor. This same combination makes an enjoyable soup or noodle dish, too.

You can also accent a dish by frying tulsi leaves gently in oil until crisp and garnishing the plate with these tasty treats. This is very similar to what I do with sage leaves (see page 166) earlier in the year. Let's combine a few of our favorite herbs for an interestingly diverse take on this technique. Tulsi, sage, mint, lemon balm, and monarda leaves can make an exciting smorgasbord of crispy flavors. Or dip the leaves in a quick tempura batter for a crunchy snack that's sure to invigorate the taste buds!

Growing and Gathering

Tulsi is a rewarding addition to the herb garden and it is quite easy to grow from seed, all you need is a little patience. Lightly cover the seeds with soil and keep them moist until germination, which can take up to 2 weeks. Once they sprout, the plants will need at least another 2 weeks of growing before you can transplant them into your garden. Be sure to wait until after any chance of frost has passed. Tulsi does well in moderate soil with full to partial sun.

You can also propagate new tulsi plants from stem cuttings or by bending branches down and partially covering them with soil. Where the stem is buried, it sets roots and then this new plant can be separated and moved to a new

The sweet, gentle flavor of tulsi blends well with local raw honey.

Tulsi Respiratory Tonic

YIELD VARIES

This herb has long been used to support respiratory health. Sprigs of freshly harvested tulsi flowers can be added to an herbal steam to break up congestion and ease a dry, scratchy cough. This is a recipe for an oxymel that can be used as a respiratory tonic. The key to this recipe is using three times more honey and vinegar than herbs.

1 part dried tulsi leaves

1 part dried plantain leaves

3 parts honey

3 parts apple cider vinegar

Combine the the herbs in a jar and cover with the honey. In a saucepan over medium heat, bring the vinegar just to a simmer, then pour it into the jar. Cap the jar and shake vigorously to mix well. Remove the cap and let the concoction cool to room temperature. Cover and let steep for about 2 weeks, shaking the jar whenever you remember.

To strain, place the closed jar in a pot of hot water to soften the honey, then strain out the herbs. Enjoy 1 teaspoon to 1 tablespoon of the oxymel whenever you feel the need. Add it to hot tea in winter or cold water in summer.

Soothing Tulsi Tea

YIELD VARIES

The simplest way to enjoy holy basil is in a soothing cup of tea. With a bit of honey and some lemon, this tasty brew will melt away the stress of the day. I find that the flavor of tulsi pairs quite well with chamomile, another relaxing friend that can join our little tea party. Not only is this infusion delightful hot, but you can also make an iced version to help you find your center during the heat of summer. Let's add some linden to the mix for a truly calming brew.

2 parts fresh tulsi leaves

1 part fresh linden flowers

½ part fresh chamomile
    flowers

Hot water, for steeping

Honey, for sweetening

Combine herbs in a tea pot and fill it with hot—just below boiling—water. Cover and let the tea brew for about 10 minutes. Serve with honey and enjoy with friends.

In warmer climates, tulsi can be grown as a perennial.

location in the garden or potted up to enjoy indoors. Indoor plants will need to be set in a south-facing window or under lights.

You can harvest leaves from tulsi anytime throughout the growing season, but ideally before the plants flower for optimum flavor. Pinch back the flower buds, as needed, to prolong the season, but once most of your crop insists on flowering, take a large harvest to dry and enjoy throughout winter. Leave some of the plants behind to finish their flowering cycle to collect seeds for planting next year.

I dry my tulsi on screens until the leaves crumble when rubbed between my fingers. I'll then strip the leaves from the stems and store them in airtight containers. The dried stems can be tossed into a campfire or burned like incense; they are quite fragrant. They can also be added to the coals of a cookfire for a fun and flavorful way to make use of these leftover sticks.

A THOUGHT TO END WITH

One of the wonderful side effects of working with herbs from a seasonal point of view is gaining greater awareness of the cyclical nature of everything around us. We experience the life cycles of the plants as we move through the seasons, but we can also see a similar progression in each individual day. Early morning plays the role of spring as life begins once again, fresh and new. Summer can be found at noon when the sun is at its highest point in the sky. We move from there into autumn as twilight quickly approaches, and winter is when we rest, reflecting on the day that has passed and the spring morning that will soon follow.

We also see these same seasons reflected in the stages of life. I suppose I'm now approaching the autumn days of my life here on Earth, but I understand that the encroaching winter does not represent the end, but merely a transition into a new beginning. The seeds that I'm planting now will ensure that new life persists in some form after I am gone. Maybe some of those very seeds are sprinkled throughout the pages of this book. With a little care and attention, they might grow to become great things.

Remember, your herbal journey will last a lifetime. With each passing season you will learn and grow, adapt, and change. This is the natural way of things. What you might find challenging now will become routine with some practice. Struggles and adversity are part of the process. These are the natural forces that push adaptation and evolution forward. If you face hardships, have no fear. Take comfort in knowing that this season will return once again, and when it does, you will have grown. You will be ready. You are a force of Nature.

There really is no difference between the herb and the herbalist. We move together in tandem on our journey through life. It's not that we're learning to work more closely *with* Nature...we *are* Nature and we're learning to work more closely with ourselves.

ACKNOWLEDGMENTS

There are many people without whom this book might never have come to be. I owe them all more than I can offer in this brief passage, but I'll try to make the most of this space.

To my team at Timber Press: Andrew, Will, Makenna, and Sarah; thank you for believing in me and the dream I had that eventually became this book.

To my amazing photographer, Miriam, for capturing the essence of each herb as it made its journey through the seasons. Your steady eye and persistent vision shine through in every photograph.

To all the herbalists who have shared their time and knowledge with me throughout the years. There are too many to name here, but to each of you, I owe a debt of gratitude.

To my dear friend, Kimberly; your songs remind me of the power that words can carry, especially when those words come from a place of love.

To my amazing sons, Elijah and Anakin; you always help me see the wonders of this world. Thank you for filling my days with joy.

To my beautiful wife, Heather; you are the rock that anchors my soul throughout the storms of life. Thank you for always being there for me and for letting me be your rock whenever you need me to be.

And to you, the reader; without you, this book would never need to exist. I hope that within these pages you find wonder and curiosity for the natural world. I hope that what I have shared with you here is valuable and that this book can serve as a guide on your journey. What is written within these pages is my love letter to Mother Nature and the herbs she so abundantly shares with us all.

PHOTO CREDITS

SUGGESTED READING

As you continue your journey, here's a selection of wonderful books that further explore ways to work with herbs in the kitchen, garden, or apothecary. It was impossible to curate a complete list, as there are so many titles to choose from, but here are a few of the books I've found to be valuable companions.

Creating Sanctuary by Jessi Bloom; Timber Press, 2018
This is a fun book that shows us how our gardens can help us create peace and happiness in our lives.

Gardening Without Work by Ruth Stout; Echo Point Books and Media, 2013
I recommend this book to everyone! Although it's not specifically about herbs, Stout's humorous and ingenious advice will help anyone grow a better garden, with less work!

Garlic Is Life by Chester Aaron; Ten Speed Press, 1996
While this book reads like a memoir of a garlic-obsessed gardener, Aaron's enthusiasm for the natural world, and the wonders of cultivating Earth, is contagious.

Any *Herb of the Year* book; International Herb Association
Each year, the International Herb Association publishes a book celebrating the Herb of the Year. Since 1995, they have written about some of my favorite herbs including fennel, lemon balm, parsley, rose, and savory. Each volume includes folklore and history, as well as recipes for working with each herb in the kitchen and apothecary.

The Artisan Herbalist by Bevin Cohen; New Society Publishers, 2021
If you're interested in learning more about the techniques behind crafting herbal teas, tinctures, and oils, then my book on this topic is just what you need. There's also a chapter on launching a small-scale herbal business.

The Complete Guide to Seed & Nut Oils by Bevin Cohen; New Society Publishers, 2022
Yes, it's me again. This book will show you everything you need to know to grow, forage, and press your own seed and nut oils right at home. These oils are ideal for culinary use, but also for infusing herbs to create high-quality salves, lotions, and balms.

The Nutmeg Trail by Eleanor Ford; Apollo Publishers, 2022
Although this book is more about spices than herbs, the exploration of botanical history and our relationships with these plants is fascinating. And the recipes are incredible!

The Untold History of Healing by Wolf D. Storl; North Atlantic Books, 2017
I love exploring the botanical and cultural history of plants. We can learn so much about their uses and impact on the world, and how we relate to the herbs and their stories.

Weeds in My Garden by Charles B. Heiser; Timber Press, 2003
This is a fun and informational guide to looking at the plants in our backyards just a little bit differently.

Women Healers of the World by Holly Bellebuono; Skyhorse, 2014
This incredible book is full of inspirational stories about medicine makers, herbal traditions, and healing practices from around the world.

INDEX

anxiety
    chamomile, 82
    coriander, 140
    tulsi, 235
    valerian, 181
arnica, 20–24
    growing and gathering, 23
    kitchen uses, 21, 22
    lotion, 24
    medicinal uses, 20
    topical spray, 24
Arnica chamissonis, 23
Arnica cordifolia, 20
Arnica montana, 20, 22, 23
ashwagandha, 192–194
    growing and gathering, 194
    kitchen uses, 194
    medicinal uses, 192–194
Asteraceae, 81
astragalus, 20
autumn garden, 129–130

Balm of Gilead tree, 57
balms, 13
balsam poplar, 57
bee balm, 102
beer brewing, 83
bees, 30, 61, 103, 179, 235
beeswax, 12–13
biennials, 53
black poplar, 57
blue chamomile, 82
bronze fennel, 203
bug bites
    chickweed, 31
    monarda, 102
    plantain, 108
    savory, 169
bundling herbs, 189

burns
    chickweed, 31
    cleavers, 33
    dandelion, 38
    See also sunburn
butterflies, 71, 103, 179, 181

caffeine, 33, 35
calendula, 25–29, 133, 228
    butter sauce, 29
    growing and gathering, 28
    kitchen uses, 27–28
    medicinal uses, 25, 27, 28
    tea, 29
Calendula officinalis, 25–29
Camellia sinensis, 216–219
capsaicin, 195
Capsicum annuum, 195–198
Capsicum chinese, 195, 197
Capsicum frutescens, 195
capsules, 12
Carmelite water, 92
carminatives
    coriander, 140
    dill, 41–42
    ginger, 212–213
    sage, 165
    savory, 168
carvacrol, 101, 155
carvone, 97
cassia, 199
cayenne, 133, 188, 195–198, 210
    fire cider, 51
    growing and gathering, 197–198
    joint liniment, 197
    kitchen uses, 196–197
    medicinal uses, 195–196
    warming spice blend, 198

Cerastium fontanum, 32
Ceylon cinnamon, 199, 200
Chamaemelum nobile, 81–84
chamazulene, 82
chamomile, 61, 81–84, 221, 227
    apple chamomile bread, 83
    growing and gathering, 84
    kitchen uses, 82–84
    medicinal uses, 82
    salve, 82
chickweed, 25, 30–32
    growing and gathering, 32
    kitchen uses, 31–32
    medicinal uses, 30–31
chicory, 134–138
    growing and gathering, 138
    kitchen uses, 135–138
    liver tonic, 137
    medicinal uses, 134–135
    tea, 137
Cichorium endivia, 134
Cichorium intybus, 134–138
cilantro, 139, 140–141, 142
Cinnamomum cassia, 199
Cinnamomum spp., 199–202
Cinnamomum verum, 199, 200, 202
cinnamon, 188, 199–202
    cinnamon roll bites, 201
    growing and gathering, 202
    kitchen uses, 200–202
    medicinal uses, 199–200
    tea, 201
cleavers, 33–35
    growing and gathering, 35
    kitchen uses, 34–35
    medicinal uses, 33–34
cognitive function
    ashwagandha, 192–193

Heather Cohen

BEVIN COHEN is an award-winning author, herbalist, owner of Small House Farm, and host of the popular *Seeds & Weeds* podcast. Bevin offers workshops and lectures across the country on the benefits of living closer to the land through seeds, herbs, and locally grown food. He is the author or editor of more than 10 books, including *The Artisan Herbalist* and *The Complete Guide to Seed & Nut Oils*. Learn more about Bevin's work at BevinCohen.com.